SITUATIONS
Vol. 1 Love's Never Ending Beginnings

Written by
J. Gralyn Stokes
www.jgralyn.com

SITUATIONS
Copyright © 2021 by J. Gralyn Stokes

All rights reserved. No part of this publication may be reproduced, distributed, or transmitted in any form or by any means, including photocopying, recording, or other electronic or mechanical methods, without the prior written permission of the publisher or author, except in the case of brief quotations embodied in critical reviews and certain other noncommercial uses permitted by copyright law.

Although every precaution has been taken to verify the accuracy of the information contained herein, the author and publisher assume no responsibility for any errors or omissions. No liability is assumed for damages that may result from the use of information contained within.

Library of Congress Control Number: 2021902011
ISBN-13:   Paperback: 978-1-64749-340-0
               ePub: 978-1-64749-341-7

Printed in the United States of America

GoToPublish LLC
1-888-337-1724
www.gotopublish.com
info@gotopublish.com

www.abstrakk.com
jgstokes@abstrakk.com
First Printed 2010 by Abstrakk Ink

ACKNOWLEDGEMENTS

First, I would like to thank God for giving me the strength to finally complete my dream. I have learned through this process that all things happen in your time. You are the writer of my life's story and I thank you for blessing me with an outlet to express my thoughts.

I would like to thank my entire family for supporting me and standing behind every word I have ever written. My mother, for being my solid rock and endless source of inspiration. To Shana, for being my best friend and toughest critic, no words can express how much you both mean in my life. To my father, I thank you for the tough love and continuous support. Everything I've done and try to do, come from the strength you've given me.

Brianna, it has been an absolute pleasure watching you grow into such a beautiful young lady. I will always be here for you. To my Godchildren, you are truly a blessing in my life, thank you for inspiring me to be better. To any child that I have ever had the pleasure to teach, work with or simply be close to, you have touched me more than you could ever know.

To my extended family, there are absolutely no words I can say to thank you for the support you have given me all these years. When I was down, you always encouraged me to keep pushing and never give up on my dream. Thank you so much for your loving support and friendship.

To everyone who has ever loved, supported, or doubted…thanks for the inspiration.

Many blessings

INTRODUCTION

Vol 1 is a collection of poems I wrote between 1996 and 2010. It took a while to finally put the whole project together and turning it into a 14 year journey was definitely not my intention. There was admittedly a lot of procrastination involved in the process. I could be cliché and say that everything happened in His perfect timing, but that would be a cop out. True, a lot more experiences happened in my life which enabled me to create new stories and more content. But I lacked a lot of discipline and focus during this time. Something many of us experience.

Whether it was my professional goals, love, or everyday life, it was a period of time where procrastination and fear consumed me. But I always had dreams of being published and one day having my words available to the world. I knew saying "I'll get to it tomorrow" or waiting for the perfect time wasn't going to help me get to where I wanted to be. I had seen too many examples of how tomorrow wasn't guaranteed. So one day I woke up and put away the excuses. I dedicated the summer to getting my book published.

Life happens, but allowing fear to alter your focus and desire for something greater is a tragedy in itself. You'd be surprised how many blessings and opportunities will present themselves when you take the initial step for more. I hope this book inspires you to take the first step. Put away the excuses and stop procrastinating toward your destiny.

01 Love Songs

The Proposal	02
Let's Make Love	03
Boy or Girl?	04
The Musician	05
Enchanted Lady	06
In Love	07
Sports Fan	08
Sincerely	09
Vanity's Poem	10
Mention Me	11
It's Official	12
From Here to Eternity	13
I AM	14
Appreciation	15
B4U	16
La Poesia	17
The Wedding Song	18
Imagination	19
Bye Bye Blackbird	20
Love vs. Loneliness	21
I Wish We Were Strangers	22
Wall of Silence	23
Escape	24
Drastic Measures	25
The Great Pretender	26
Her Story	27
US	28
No Doubt	29
Love is an Investment	30

02 The Storm

Reverse	**32**
Expectations	**34**
Marry Me	**36**

03 Jack Tales

Business Meeting	**38**
Last Touch	**39**
Employee Benefits	**40**
Life!	**42**
Mother Nature	**43**
Lap Dance ft. Monica Holmes	**44**
Happy Hour	**46**
3 Part Harmony	**47**
September Love	**49**

04 Love Infinite

Single Father	**52**
Dear Myrlie	**53**
1600	**54**
God Father	**55**
Grandmamma	**56**
9 Months	**57**
Little Angel	**58**
Our Father	**59**

01
Love Songs

Love is a really scary thing, and you never know what's going to happen. It's one of the most beautiful things in life, but it's one of the most terrifying. It's worth the fear because you have more knowledge, experience, you learn from people, and you have memories.

- Ariana Grande

THE PROPOSAL

I haven't slept in a week
I've been trying to find a romantic way to sweep you off your feet
But I want this to be more special than any other moment in time
I want this to be the day that will forever last in your mind
You see, these past few years you have been my heart, my soul, & my everything
You are my queen, & today I want to present to you this ring
I'm not really sure what I should do or how I should go about this
but walking down that aisle with you would be a dream. I must admit, I was so nervous
So, I called you & invited you to our private spot in the park
After all, this was the placed we first kissed...the place you stole my heart
When you arrived you were greeted with a picnic basket & a blanket covered with roses
Your beautiful eyes sparkled & it was at this moment when I felt we were the closest
I crept up behind you, held you tight & greeted you with a kiss on the cheek
The violinist playing in the background put you in the mood, the champagne made you weak
I was so nervous, I could hardly speak, but somehow I maintained
& then suddenly from the sky fell a light rain
but this didn't ruin the mood, in fact it made it better
It just showed that a love like ours could make it through any type of weather
After we ate, we just sat up all night, looking at the stars
It was our way of thanking God for blessing us with a love like ours
Then, I got on 1 knee & I asked, what you had planned for the rest of your life?
I pulled out a ring, kissed you gently & asked...
if you would be my wife

LET'S MAKE LOVE

Because you gave your heart to me
I vow to devote my love to you eternally
I want to make love…but not just any kind of love
sweet love
the love you never get tired of
amazing love
the kind that dreams are made of
musical love
like your favorite love song that stays in your head all day
peaceful love
when you know I'll never harm you in any way
religious love
when you feel the power of God blessing you every minute
spiritual love
like an angel spreading his wings, watching over with love infinite
unbreakable love
with boundaries deceit can't walk around
undying love
the kind that few people who leave this earth can ever say that they've found

Do you want to make love?

BOY OR GIRL?

candlelight dinners
hot wax
slow CDs
sit back & relax
erotic dreams fulfilled
no emotions concealed
intimacy
remarkable chemistry
passionate embrace
gentle kiss across your face
a lick around your secluded spots
simple words to make you hot
irresistible love, soothing like poetry
climactic waterfalls, you have to go down low to see
you & me
eternity
forget about the rest of the world
boy or girl?

THE MUSICIAN

Every time I'm near you, it's like hearing songs from up above
Your sweet touch makes me want to dance, every time we make love
Your voice is as soft as the sweet sounds from a violin
Silky & smooth like a soprano sax, is the best way to describe your skin
You make my heart skip more beats than any bass drum or snare
The beauty of the chords from a piano, remind me most of your hair
Always pretty, like listening to the gentle sounds of a harp
You are the director of my choir & I thank the Lord for bringing you into my heart
When we're together, it's like hearing my favorite love song
Because you make the sweetest music in the world & you can play for me all night long

ENCHANTED LADY

Just the simple look in her eyes can drive a man crazy
I am hypnotized by the beauty of this enchanted lady
I have never seen any other lips so soft or skin so smooth
Just the thought of her caress, sends me into a romantic mood
Sometimes I think of her & get lost in the moment, losing touch with reality
Wondering why this enchanted lady, has me obsessing so emphatically
Far too precious to be passed around casually,
she is a gem
Her presence alone demands the respect of any man, if she chooses to give her love to him
She is aware of her beauty, but is careful of the way she flaunts it
Independent, she knows how to get what she wants, when she wants it
Open to affection but careful with her emotions, she doesn't fall in love easily
She knows how to make love & take it, if it's not being given equally
Like a mother she takes your pain, like a sister she gives a love without measure
My enchanted lady is a queen & her love I will cherish forever

In love with...

>*your words*
>*your spirit*
>*your presence*
>*your touch*
>*your mind*
>*your body*
>*your lips*
>*your kiss*

In love with...you

SPORTS FAN

You must play on the offensive line, because you have protected me from hurt
No one has ever made such an impact on my team of love...you did it 1st
You scored the most points in a season every time you touched down on my heart
There are no penalties in this game, no out of bounds & no false starts
You lead the league in forced turnovers, by intercepting all of my fears
The team doctor keeps us strong, to ensure our love has a lasting career
You made the all-defensive team when you sacked my pain & tackled all of my worries
You have done more than rewrite the record book of my heart, you have started a whole new story
I thank God for being our coach & calling all the right plays
I don't think the critics thought our chemistry, would come together this way
You are the M.V.P. of my life, a certified All-Star
You took us to the Super Bowl when nobody picked us to make it this far
I became a better receiver, when I began to catch your kiss
I was the worst kicker in the league until you joined my team, now I can't miss
You have taken the starting position in my life, a leader who is calm under pressure
We carry the championship ring of love, the ring that signifies we will be together forever

SINCERELY

You are the Allie to my Noah within
All space & time our love transcends
No distance, nor trial can keep us away
Your eyes are the notebook that tells our story, I read you everyday
You are the end of the inconsistency of love past
Our love is a Hollywood feature film & you my dear, are star of the cast
There is no astronomical event or crisis we can't rise above
No natural disaster could match this outpouring of love, not even a tsunami's flood
I never knew I would find a love so good it would make breathing a difficult task
I try to be discreet with my emotions, but my feelings for you, are impossible to mask
So what more could I ask? Personality with beauty beyond description
I could circle the entire globe & never find a more stunning vision
You embody everything that I desire in a woman
Beauty, strength & independence
     damn...you make it hard for me to function
From now until forever your happiness is my sole objective
Your pain is my pain, I will never leave you neglected
We are like two athletes running stride for stride, only God knows how this race will end
But I am so grateful to have you by my side. My wife, my lover, my friend

VANITY'S POEM

No matter how I'm feeling, you brighten up my day
In the storm & rain you push the clouds away
In sinking sand you help me to stand
When I lose confidence, you make me a better man
You are the 1 I wish I could have,
But I don't mind taking walks with you down Friendship Ave.
When my days don't go right, you show me the light
When I run out of ink, you bring new life to the words I write
You have a beauty that cannot be measured
Eyes like pearls of a priceless treasure
Caramel skin as soft as cotton
You passed me like the wind, but your image cannot be forgotten
Sexy with class & intelligence to match
Able to bring sunshine to my day, when I am blessed to cross your path
You give me the words when I am unable to speak
& no matter who I love, or who I am with, you will always make me weak

MENTION ME

I know that the time we had together was only for a moment
but that's all it took for you to change life for me as I know it
I think about you all the time & my friends are starting to think I'm weird
but I only started going crazy the moment you disappeared
I know there's a very slim chance that we'll ever see each other again
but I'm going to think positive & hope that we could become friends
Because I am shy, I let you slip right out of my hands,
but I pray every night, I get a second chance to be your man
Yeah, I know that it's wishful thinking & probably a long shot
but that's what I'm going to hold on to, because that's all I've got
I don't know what kind of impression I gave you, or how you feel about me
but what you gave me is something I thought I'd never feel or ever get to see
If we never see each other again, I guess it wasn't meant to be
But I'll keep praying so when asked "Who's your man?", you can mention me.

IT'S OFFICIAL

It's official, you have me grinning from ear to ear
My heart would love to accompany your soul for the rest of my years
You turn me on in every way imaginable, just the simple look in your eyes
I get the chills just thinking of you, you give me constant butterflies
I have never been happier, you are the joy that healed my hurt
You are the reason I believe there is heaven on earth
You showed me a place, where time stands still
A place where true love is revealed
A place, where tears of joy are the only tears you cry
A place where the stars sparkle like glitter in the sky
I love going to sleep, knowing there's a possibility I'll see you in my dreams
It's a blessing knowing I will wake up with you beside me, loving me with your every being
Your ring signifies the undying & faithful love that I have for you
You return that love & commitment to me, even though you don't have to
You will forever be a part of my life, wherever I go or whatever I choose to do
I can no longer hide the fact, that I'm officially crazy over you

FROM HERE TO ETERNITY

Though our love is close, the distance is driving us apart
You are the 1 I love most, but I can't stop this lonely feeling in my heart
I can't stand not being able to see you & hold you close to me
I just wish we could be together, like a relationship is supposed to be
The day we met, we were both away from our homes
A short period of time, that left a welcome chill in my bones
Just by the look in your eyes, I knew what we had was magic
but I'm afraid the distance might make this beautiful thing we have seem tragic
Maybe I'm jumping to conclusions, maybe distant lovers are something we could learn to be
but until then please know, that you could turn to me from here to eternity

I AM

I am your first love
I am your first broken heart
I am the stars in the sky
I am your light when it's dark
I am what makes you smile
I am what drives you wild
I am joy
I am pain
I am sunshine
I am rain
I am that sweet voice
I am what makes lips moist
I am the words to your favorite song
I am peace when things go wrong
I am love at first sight
I am the tears that last all night
I am the forbidden love you can't refuse
I am the once in a lifetime love you don't want to lose
I am the arms that keep you warm
I am the feeling of holding your first born
Who am I?

I AM INSPIRATION

APPRECIATION

Just a simple hello
A simple smile to let me know
An unexpected phone call
Holding hands in the mall
A nice compliment
The smell of a rose's scent
Breakfast in bed
The words, "I love you" being said
A kiss before you leave
All help me to believe

I am appreciated

B4U

Sometimes love will break your heart & at times can be very stressful
but no matter the hurt or heartache I went through, I always dreamed I'd find someone special
Before you, I was starting to think that this love thing was lame
but the day God brought you into my life, all of that changed
You were the 1st to not take advantage of my heart & try to play games
You, you are the fire that allows my soul to maintain
I can't imagine a beautiful picture without you in the frame
I can't imagine living life without you, it just wouldn't be the same
All the arguments we had in the past, I guess we were both to blame
But yet in still, I apologize for anything I did to cause you pain
I'm usually calm & cool but without you I go insane
When I'm around you, it's hard to keep the animal inside of me tame
Do you remember the 1st time you came?
Or the 1st time you yelled my name?
Our hearts were synchronized & our bodies lit a flame
The softest place on earth is where my love took aim
Like any other relationship, we will go through the sunshine & the rain
But to say that I found a love greater than yours, is 1 thing I'll never be able to claim

LA POESÍA

I don't remember exactly how we met
nor did I realize that your presence would leave such a lasting effect
I've told you all of my deepest secrets, all of which you've kept
I told you about all of my dreams after every night that I slept
You were always there to listen to me, even when those nights grew long
We never had an argument & you loved me whether I was right or wrong
I see men & women trying to talk, walk…just be in your presence
With everybody trying to get at you, it's hard not to get jealous
I never had a problem with you going both ways because you always saved a little piece of your day to listen to what I had to say
You gave me a voice in which to speak my mind
You helped me realize my silence is not divine
You were my friend through some of the hardest times
You helped me up the mountain, when I didn't think I would be able to climb
You know I will still call you when I finally find the 1
Hopefully, we'll still be in contact the day I have my son or daughter, either way I'll feel blessed
I pray I will never have to experience missing your lyrical caress
You are my words, you are my song & I have fallen for you
You speak for my silence & represent my courage, when they are absent I call for you
My sweet Poesía, this poem is dedicated to you
Our relationship was written, only God can separate us 2

THE WEDDING SONG

To you my sweet, I vow true love forever
I'll be there for you through any weather, for worse or for better
You are the only 1, who has truly captured my heart
that's why I plan to be with you till death do us part
I never thought that I would ever get to see this day
or even dreamed that I could possibly feel this way
You have gotten rid of my darkness on the outside
& filled me with happiness on the inside
Webster has yet to find the word that could accurately define my feelings for you
Wedding gown, tux, family & friends…my dream has finally come true
This is our day & our new life begins now
& until the day I die, I promise to stand by these vows

                                                love always…

IMAGINATION

How would you feel if I touched your...
I love how you make your tongue go across my...
Music is playing in the background as we...
The incense is an aphrodisiac,
it adds to the passion as I go down...
It's intense the way you react,
it makes me work harder to find your...
We have so much fun when we start to...
The job is not done until we've both reached our...
Your body begins to shiver, every time we...
You wake up in the morning, after a long beautiful night of...
An orgasmic vacation, you were taken away from a world filled with...
When you return, your friends see you beaming as you go back to the...
You never give a detail of what took place
you simply tell them to use their....

BYE BYE BLACKBIRD

You make me feel good every time I see you
A walking fantasy, is it possible mine has finally come true?
I blush when I receive your text
We decided to wait, so these emotions are bigger than sex
Every time I hear the harmony of your voice,
it gives me confirmation that I've made the right choice
You make me want to do better,
you spark the light in my soul when we're together
I waited so long for you, though you have always existed in my mind
I get jealous of your shadow, because it gets to be in your presence at all times
You brought me a love that most people have prayed for their whole lives,
a love people read about & only see researching the historical archives
We seem so perfect for each other,
if it's possible, I think I've found the perfect lover
We are friends first,
my emotions are about to burst...
So why am I expecting the worst?
Possibly because my previous loves have been cursed
Maybe this curse is self-imposed
Inexperienced with love, maybe sometimes I force the doors to close
You see when the 1st thing goes wrong I get scared
It's as if I start finding excuses & give love a reason not to be there
Too often, I push love away
& cut off any chance of convincing it to stay
But I don't want to do that with you,
I don't want this ridiculous cycle to continue
My beautiful blackbird, don't spread your wings & fly away from me
Let me be the wind beneath your wings & I will fly with you through eternity

LOVE VS. LONELINESS

A constant battle goes on in my mind
A distorted pattern, I lay awake trying to figure out the designs
I was told Love was patient, but I've seen 1st hand that Loneliness is persistent
I see people blessed with Love, who lose it all because they never truly understood Commitment
I have grown quite familiar with Loneliness, we've actually become good friends
It leaves me to wonder when my relationship with Love is going to begin
but I try to find Patience, because that's what everybody says I'm supposed to do
but they've probably never experienced what being close to Loneliness can do to you
As for Love, if you only knew how true I would be
So compassionate & faithful, you would feel completely comfortable & safe with me
I see you walk past me & sometimes I let you go
Why, I don't know, Shyness usually walks in uninvited & interrupts my flow
Confidence is so inconsistent, he's like a revolving door
Some days he's by my side, some days he's not. I'm never really sure
I would really like to meet Faith, then I would have no worries at all
Because with her, I would realize it is out of my hands,
& that Heaven is the only place Love will fall
I've talked to a few of my friends, some of them are fighting the same fight,
though we wake with Loneliness, we pray for Love every night.

I WISH WE WERE STRANGERS

I wish I could go back into time
When your presence was a mystery in my mind
When our souls had yet to meet
& the thought of seeing you would make me weak
The times I would wake up early just to get a glimpse of your face
Daydreaming about the beautiful child we could one day create
But who could've predicted my fate?
Everything you ask for, may not be the right thing for you
In order to build a castle of love, you must first have the proper tools
If we were strangers, you could have never broken my heart or led me astray
There are certain rules to being in love, that you chose to disobey
While you're feeling like everything is okay,
I'm wishing I could go back into time
When your presence was a mystery in my mind
But was this all part of God's design?
Could you have been a test to prepare me for the next stranger in line?
Some say love is blind & this I choose to believe
Because for now love, you are still a stranger, who has yet to introduce herself to me

WALL OF SILENCE

When I'm alone, my feelings for you are clear & coherent,
but when I'm next to you, I can't seem to make them apparent
Right now, I feel invisible in your eyes, I wish you could know the real me
Every day I see you is like watching the sunrise, I pray seeing the sunrise with you could 1 day be my reality
I can only imagine my lips against yours, my tongue massaging your flesh
my feelings getting harder for you every second, just watching you undress.
If only I could find the words to make our souls connect... maybe 1 day I will,
for it would be tragic for this passion to remain concealed
But I know someday it will be revealed, "This is what I say every morning I wake"
but in your presence, there is a wall of silence, that I am unable break

ESCAPE

I don't know why you decide to let him take you on this ride
When will you realize, that real love & hard punches will never coincide?
He'll never know the person that I know inside
He'll never give you the things a real love should provide
What is he thinking? Are you supposed to bow down to his every need after he's finished drinking?
Meanwhile your soul is sinking & those last blows are preventing your eyes from blinking
You can't even cry, why do you listen to him lie?
Behind every scar is a painful truth, even he can't deny
To make up for him throwing you around,
he takes you out for a night on the town
& as he looks at the asses, of every girl that passes
You are forced to wear sunglasses, to hide the scratches from the masses
A love like this is disastrous, or can you really call it love?
He hits you with his fist on the mattress, then he goes to the club
You are too beautiful to be hurting
You can come with me if you need a place to stay
But I can't live another day, knowing that your heart is in dismay
Other than that, I don't know what else I can say
All I can do is pray you find the strength to get away

DRASTIC MEASURES

The day you left, it felt like a door being slammed in my face
because I couldn't imagine living with someone else filling your space
The day you left, all the joy in my life went away
because it didn't seem possible to see another happy day
The day you left, all the money in the world wouldn't have made any sense
because I refuse to believe the life we had is now in the past tense
The day you left, it seemed as if my whole life came to an end
It felt as if I was living in an imaginary world & I could no longer pretend
The day you left, I had a feeling of emptiness in my heart, because I had never thought I would see the day we'd be apart
The day you left, I knew there was no way I could ever forget you
That's when I decided to take drastic measures to be with you...

THE GREAT PRETENDER

Every time I'm with you I try to pretend
that your heart is truly with me & not with him
The time I spend with you is truly a blessing,
but in terms of my heart, I don't know if it's the best thing
As we grow closer, it will be more difficult for us to fall apart
& I don't know if what I'm feeling will be worth the pain in my heart
I know you have feelings for me & I have feelings for you too
but you have a lot more to lose than me, so who am I to pressure you
Even if you were to leave for me, I don't want to have to believe
That the time we spend is just an easier way for you to grieve
Oh what a tangled web we weave...
Why is it for your love I live & breathe?
Why is it fate has chosen our souls to meet now?
If there is a way that we could be together, I want to know how
It's hard for me to hate him, because he doesn't even know what we're doing
I blame destiny for bringing us together, knowing we were destined to be ruined
I don't want to be around you anymore, because I can no longer pretend
You need to decide if your heart is with me or if it truly belongs to him

HER STORY

How much farther do we have to climb?
How much longer will we play with time?
I have given my everything to you,
my life, my love & a beautiful child too
How many more rivers do we have to cross?
How long will I remain in this, in love…lost?
What more must I do to show you how I feel is real?
What is keeping you from making the proposal that will close the deal?
You say it's not me
You say you're happy
You say you need time
I'm losing my mind
When I say it's over, you don't want me to leave
but if I stay, you don't do anything to make me believe
I don't know how much longer I can go on feeling this way
I want to settle down & be with you the rest of my days
I will do anything in my power to try & keep what we have together
but I can't wait around forever, it has to be now or never

US

I need to call a cardiologist
maybe he can help my heart adjust
At times I feel as if my mind is going to bust
We used to get goose bumps every time we touched
How can you say we had nothing? Like we don't have anything to discuss
There was a time when I warmed your soul. Do I now fill it with disgust?
Did we ever really have a relationship built on trust?
It seems as if our love of steel is now covered with rust
We used to be able to talk about anything, now all we do is fuss
I thought it was love, but maybe it was all lust
For 2 people who were so meant to be, how is it that we ended up crushed?
So wrapped up & caught in the moment…
we couldn't figure out what went wrong between, us

NO DOUBT

No doubt, your love was the sweetest thing I've ever known
Without your love, I wouldn't have been able to manage on my own
No doubt, the fellas used to get jealous when they saw you with me
Baby, my whole world stopped every time you kissed me
No doubt, you were too fly for the human eye, you stayed on my mind
You could make me see if I was blind, thinking about you took up all my time
No doubt, I would've given you my ear if you needed it to hear
I would've given you both my eyes if it would've helped you see more clear
No doubt, you were my heart & I was pumping nothing but love for you
Sometimes, I had to stop & just thank the man up above for you
No doubt, our love was something everybody else dreamed about
So tell me, love, why the hell did you kick me out?

LOVE IS AN INVESTMENT

What is the key to maintaining a relationship, does anybody really know?
How do you know when you've found true love or determine when it's time to let go?
Why is it that love is so beautiful & overwhelming in the beginning,
but you are never really able to determine the reasons behind its ending?
How is it we go from singing "nothing really matters" & "never gonna let you go"
to singing "missing you" & always ending up with "1 last cry" when nights are cold?
Why do walks on the beach, candlelit dinners, & romantic poems lose their value?
When does 3:00 AM convo, an unexpected rose, or a "just to say hi" phone call no longer do?
"I've finally found the 1" or "we will be together forever" is always the 1st thing you say,
but it so easily becomes "I don't know what went wrong" or "how did things end up this way?"
How is it people can spend half their lives together, both physically & mentally,
only to find out that the love they knew, wasn't really meant to be?
Could it be that they were always aware, but were simply afraid to be alone?
Or maybe they are too afraid to leave the only home they've ever known
Whatever the reason, love is but a journey, another 1 of life's tests
So we must take our time when investing in love, in order to find true happiness

02
The Storm

The most beautiful people we have known are those who have known defeat, known suffering, known struggle, known loss, and have found their way out of those depths.

- Elisabeth Kubler-Ross

REVERSE

What if you could go back in time, knowing what you know now?
If you could reverse your mistakes & take advantage of missed opportunities, wouldn't you want to know how?
I wish someone would invent a time machine,
so I could go back & explore moments unseen
I would reverse time with a mature mind
press rewind to the *maybes* & hit eject to all the *what ifs* left behind
If the opportunity presented itself to you,
What would you do?

Wouldn't you have appreciated her more & told her you loved her every day if you had known she was going to die?
Wouldn't you have remained true & faithful, if you had known the grass wasn't as green on the other side?
Would you have allowed him to take so much of your soul, if you knew he had no intention of giving you his?
Wouldn't you have chosen the 1 who was willing to love you, instead of repeatedly choosing the 1's who never did?

Hmm...what would I do?

I would've grabbed her & kissed her, like she had never been kissed before
I would've been more aggressive, so she would have been undoubtedly sure
I would have made my feelings known, so that it wouldn't have been a mystery
Who knows? She may have become overjoyed & over loved over me
I would have valued their presence more, while they were here
I wouldn't skip an opportunity to say "I love you," knowing those precious moments would soon disappear
I would go back & eliminate the procrastination in my life & push harder to accomplish my goals
I wouldn't give energy to those who hurt me, or worry about the things I couldn't control...

The thing is, there will never be a time machine & we will never be able to reverse the past
We could waste precious moments trying to rewrite history, but in doing so, we keep the blessings of the future in overcast
Our time machine is experience & our testimony is our 2nd chance
In order to grow & become a better person, we must take something from each circumstance
God is the timekeeper, navigator, & manager, in life's journey we travel each day
It hurts Him when we complain & grumble about life & lose faith that he will take our pain away
So regardless of the mistakes, lost loves, or what could have been
We must live & embrace each moment as precious & make sure those same mistakes never happen again

EXPECTATIONS

Why do we put such high expectations on love, yet expect so little from ourselves?
We expect love to just fall into our laps & when it comes, we immediately expect it to fail
Sometimes we want things when we want them whether it's right for us or not
We are sometimes so consumed by what we think we need, that we neglect to take care of the things we got
Why do we try to change someone to fit our image of them, only to find ourselves unhappy with the results?
You can never truly be happy with the image you created, because a counterfeit image has no true pulse
How can we expect to see greater results in life, if we don't aspire to reach for greatness?
We want God to immediately fix our problems, yet we don't display patience
So much of life goes wasted
Time is something you never get back, we must view each second as sacred
We cannot expect our situation to change, without 1st changing our attitude
We have to stop complaining about what we don't have & embrace what we do with gratitude
That rejected job promotion,
the career that never got set into motion,
that relationship that just wouldn't work,
the 1 you tried to save, no matter how badly it made you hurt,
the goal that seemed impossible to attain,
the long lost love you were never able to claim...
Maybe it just wasn't your time
Sometimes failure & disappointment are a sign
God has a way of denying or giving you exactly what you ask for
Just so you can appreciate what you have or what is about to come even more
Expect to have a great day every day you are blessed to see the sunrise
Live life expecting good things to happen & don't let life's distractions take your eyes off the prize...

View each breath as a new opportunity
to achieve your goals & dreams
Live life with high expectations & go through your journey
with a full head of steam

MARRY ME

I'm going to take a little time to take care of me
The disappointments of the heart seem unfair & hard to believe
Every time I break down & decide to give love another chance,
I always seem to end up doing the same old dance
Just when I begin to think things are starting to go right, they go wrong
I don't think I can handle dealing with any more pain in my life, I don't think I'm that strong
My heart's not ready to go through anymore hurt
I don't think it's selfish of me, to want to put me 1st
Maybe in the future I'll be able to lift this curse
Eventually I'll find someone who is able to prove their worth
Until that time, I'm doing me
Here's my chance to get my life together, I will embrace the opportunity
No one can love me better than me, self-love doesn't require anybody else
I don't need anyone to make me feel miserable, I can do bad all by myself
God promised He would send me that special gem
It is my job to prepare myself & remain obedient to Him
So when that time comes I will be able to exhale in the moment
I will be stronger & much wiser, so when love knocks I will know it
I will be ready to take love head on, if she hurts me I will be just fine
If it happens, it happens. If it doesn't, it obviously wasn't in God's design
Love will no longer have the power to break me, nor will it take my will
Love is not fake or hurtful & I won't settle until true love is revealed
So for right now I'm chilling, going to take a little time to take care of me
Minus the ring & the ceremony, it's time to marry "me"

03
Jack Tales

Everyone has a different life story. Things happen rapidly for someone, and things move slowly for others.

— Barun Sobti

BUSINESS MEETING

I'm thinking thoughts I shouldn't be thinking...I'm a married man. Falling in love with you, was definitely not in the plans. I would always see you in Atlanta at our quarterly business meetings, those boring conferences with CEOs, that took up the whole weekend. I showed you pictures of my kids & even bragged about my wife. I told you how beautiful she was & how she brought so much joy to my life. But what was it about that night? Before I left, me & my baby had just had a fight. Anger & frustration clouded my mind the entire flight. Suddenly, every word you said seemed so right.
A couple of drinks, a lot of laughs, a kiss...my first mistake. Me, you, a hotel room...I can't believe what has just taken place.
I started flying to quarterly business meetings, monthly, & then weekly. The ninth cloud kept me from seeing my family beneath me. The more distant I grew, the quicker my wife put together 2 & 2. She never said it, but deep down, I think she always knew. But she never left me... to save us, she did everything she could do. She went above & beyond. Dinners, massages & the loving was never better. But I just couldn't resist temptation, no matter how hard she fought to keep us together. You would think me seeing her strength could help me overcome my weakness. I couldn't even see that I was taking advantage of her sweetness. On my last meeting, I went to break the whole thing off; my conscience was killing me. I told her I needed to get my life together & that our relationship could no longer be.
When I got back home, my wife & kids were not there. There was a note in the bathroom by the mirror where she did her hair. The note read, "I have to be honest, this past year I have been cheating. I would always feel so lonely every time you went to another meeting. I tried to wine & dine you. I even tried harder to romance you, because I knew you were my true heaven sent. But every time you came back from a trip, you just seemed even more distant. I know your distance is all because of me. I wish I could've been the wife you wanted me to be. But baby, my conscience will no longer allow me to be dishonest, so I have to let you know. I love you too much to keep breaking your heart, so I feel it's best for me to go."

LAST TOUCH

So beautiful, even in your time of passing
I had visions our love would be everlasting
I guess now those visions can't be, but I'm not mad at you
Where you're going, there is nothing but happiness & all your dreams can come true
We've known each other for most of our lives & we knew this day would come
I just didn't want to believe your illness would take over so quickly, especially in someone so young
I'm crying right now, looking for these words
I think this is hurting me more than it's hurting you
but you are being so strong, I feel bad I'm not able to do the same for you too
Don't worry about Destinee; I know I will have plenty of help
I just never thought I would have to raise our daughter by myself
Every little girl needs her mother
I have to be honest, I am so afraid
I don't know how to be the perfect father
I know many mistakes will be made
But I just want to tell you, that I am going to miss you so much
I will never forget the first time I kissed you or the first time we touched
What we have is more than lust, it is a connection that is deeply engrained
It is difficult to hide my tears & smile, acting as if I'm not in pain
But in your last hour, I do not want to appear weak
I want "I love you" to be the last words you hear me speak
So as I give you this last kiss on the cheek,
remember that I will always be here with you, even in your sleep

EMPLOYEE BENEFITS

It was not supposed to happen this way, the penalties of recreational lust
We were just friends with benefits who liked to play, there was definitely no intention of things getting serious
You were my stress reliever when I needed to release some tension,
my part time savior who came to release me of my inhibitions
My man knows you but he was never aware,
that I chose you when he acted like he didn't care
It was cool, because both sides understood their role, we were each other's temporary fix
We were able to keep our feelings under control, a private escape, where drama didn't exist

Until now...

You see, for a week now I've been late & I don't mean late for work
My most consistent friend has never made me wait, maybe a day or 2 at the worst
I bought the pregnancy test today, I had never been more anxious in my life
I was so terrified to read what it had to say, you could have cut the tension with a knife
So I walked in the bathroom & closed the door, alone with me & my thoughts
What I saw nearly put me on the floor, reality hit me like a ton of rocks
But the story between these little blue lines, read eternity well, at least 18 years
& I am suddenly looking at my future with uncertainty, trying to avoid breaking into tears
I know it's not his, we haven't been together in months
I am not ready for any kids, but this is a reality I wasn't ready to confront

Was I ready for...

9 months of hell
my stomach starting to swell
baby names
20 hours of labor pain
dirty diapers
all nighters
ABC's
new responsibilities?

Hell no!!

I have unintentionally altered my fate
It was your touch I could never tell no, it was that touch that has me in this horrified state
So, my dear friend with benefits, how beneficial is this news to you?
How will your wife react once she knows you're not so innocent, when she's aware of the secret things we do?
She thinks we're just good friends on the job, but she's unaware that you are my star employee
She never questioned or thought our relationship was odd, but she was oblivious to the work you actually did for me
So where do we go from here? We have to put our heads together
I know our futures are now seemingly unclear, but we now share a bond that will exist forever
No more conference room quickies or extended lunch breaks, this situation just got real
Should we be honest, or do whatever it takes, to keep this thing concealed?
That was a stupid question, I know it will eventually be impossible to keep this hidden
I ride him constantly for all of his dirt & indiscretion, but for this, I don't know if I'll ever be forgiven
But he will have to make that decision, at the end of the day, I don't want him to leave
Neither of us ever intended or dreamed of being in this position, but we are now confronted with the consequences of trying to deceive

LIFE!

I was hoping that somehow, the gun blast would wake me from this dream, but that wasn't the case. I was still there breathing, my heart was still beating, & I was looking down at her face. She was looking at me too, her eyes told the story, that her mouth could no longer speak. I kept telling her to get up, but she couldn't hear me, she was fast asleep. I wonder what she was dreaming, she always said I never took her out. Maybe she was dreaming of that vacation she was always talking about. I don't know.

The blast did, however, bring me back to reality though. What the hell had I done? I never wanted to see her suffer, but this way is better for everyone. Why did she have to cheat on me? I gave her everything a woman could want, but she walked around pretending to love me... why did she feel like she had to front? Just the thought of seeing her with him...grrrh! I had my suspicions for quite some time. Those suspicions, in turn, served as the flame that sparked the fire in my clouded mind.

Maybe I didn't love her, the way she needed to be loved. Maybe some nights, I did stay out a little too late. She told me her dreams, but I never listened, she always said we never knew how to communicate. I guess she felt as if she could no longer wait, & he gave her things that I never could. She kept it quiet, because she knew I would never let her leave me, she knew I never would. But when I came home & saw them in a warm embrace, my whole body went numb. I saw the smile she put on that other man's face & just as he was about to...

All I remember was the blast, your honor, I didn't waste a single bullet in the gun. I was in such a rage, I didn't even realize the damage I had done. But I am truly sorry & I know the act I've committed, I can never take back. But I told her, no matter what it would take, I would do anything to keep our love intact.

LIFE!!

MOTHER NATURE

There's nothing more peaceful than watching clouds cry
Or watching the sun peek through to dry their eyes
Oh how I wish that I could fly
Just to discover the mysteries of the world beyond the sky
Every day here, is another day I wake & wonder if I will die
Another day to watch freedom pass me by
Tuesday was the day we were put on sale for the highest bidder to buy
He promised he would keep our family together, but that was a lie
He would take my innocence without permission, every time he touched my thigh
I had to lie there & take it, because I would be beaten if I were to ask why
When my brother tried to escape he was hung & burned, we all watched him die
He was made an example, just in case any of us wanted to try
He said we were lucky, because anything we needed he supplied
Justifying to himself that our rights weren't being denied
But my civilization doesn't seem so civilized
Each day I wake knowing my American dream will never be realized
But there's still nothing more peaceful than watching clouds cry
I pray for the day the sun comes through & dries my eyes

LAP DANCE
co-written by Monica Holmes

I was just supposed to be hanging out with my friends
My boy was getting married & we were celebrating his last free weekend
After downing a few drinks & a few lap dances, you walked in out of nowhere
You fit every physical description I desired. From your legs, to your silky smooth hair
At first you danced for my friend, but you were looking at me the whole time
I just waited for you to finish with him, I wanted you to be all mine
The sign at the door says Do Not Touch, but I couldn't keep my hands off of your flesh
I asked you if you liked the way I rubbed my hands on your breast & with no hesitation, you said yes
But I'm a realist, I know you get paid to master the art of deception
You are supposed to make me believe your intentions are sincere when u look in my direction
But something seemed different about this dance
Something was different about the way...

I move
I dance, I entice
I allow you to follow me
Your desires are transformed when you see my long mane
Once I take hold
You will never be the same
My dance is more than lap movements;
I become the beat
You become my heat
Feeln every inch of me keeps you at attention
You wanna hold back, I'm just supposed to be entertainment
My deception
My mood
My lips
My hips move, up & down
I see lust in your face...
It's ok, she doesn't have 2 know
I'm available at any moment to be your...

live fantasy
something I could never get at home
I'm loving every inch of your caress, you send chills through every bone
Your movements send a rush through my body, I'm finding it hard 2 keep control
I'm watching you, watching me, pretending you are sliding up & down my pole
This is only temporary, though I never want this moment to end
Our bodies become more in sync, such a beautiful sin
Will I ever be forgiven? I guess I'll never know
But I won't worry about that now

Shhhh…
Let me take the lead
Your thoughts
Back to me
Nothing can stop this flow
One nite with the guys
Turns into every weekend with
Me…..
Pulling, kissing
Every song turns into new ways
Look how my body do thangs
Booty bounces to your beat
Curly locks keep your attention
Desire
Me
I dance for you
I relax
You
That is
Until she walked in…

HAPPY HOUR

It had been a long & stressful week
so a few co-workers & I decided to go out for drinks
I started out with a Jack & Coke
I forgot all about my stress after a Long Island & a couple of jokes
Suddenly, the bartender passes me a note...
& said, "this is from the young lady sitting at the end of the bar
she saw you sitting here & wants to know who you are."
She was with a friend & both were very attractive to the eye
As I came over to speak, her friend moved over in the chair to the side
She had an innocence about her & her confidence intrigued me
She said, "I have never been so forward or aggressive, though you probably don't believe me."
She was right, I didn't believe her, but I played along
Perhaps her inhibitions were down or maybe that 2nd Cosmo was a little strong
We ended up talking forever about life, religion, love, & pain
& then I realized that I had never even asked her her name
So I asked, after ordering another round & our empty glasses were being taken away
She said "My name is...& you must be my new today"
I paused for a moment, because I wasn't sure what she was trying to say
She said her horoscope told her that yesterday was gone & to put the past away
"When I saw you come in...I instantly knew
that my new today, would begin with you
Don't ask me how I know, because I can't explain."
I couldn't tell if she was sincere or if the Patrón was making her light in the brain,
But I have to admit, I felt something too
I told her, "I never thought going out for drinks would bring me to someone like you,
but I am very happy we were able to cross paths...
I can't wait to see what happens next.
Cheers to our new today & many more hours of happiness!"

3 PART HARMONY

It was totally irresistible, you finally got a taste of love for the 1st time
Was it love or was it really just lust that had you going out of your mind?
Knowing you could never pull out,
you gave her something you knew she wouldn't forget about
You were the man for that instant
The furthest thing from your mind was any type of commitment
Both of you stepped into it, without a clue of what you were doing,
but once you started, it felt like a moment you believed nothing could ruin
You knew her father was on the way home,
but you were to distracted by the moans
And when he saw you with his daughter,
he tried to shoot you with the gun he owned
A few weeks later, you get a call on the phone
The voice on the other end brought a serious change to your tone
"You about to be a daddy" she replied
Nothing could explain the fear you felt inside
You tried to come up with any excuse to make this nightmare seem untrue
but she had never been with anyone either, it was her 1st time too
Your mind was racing, "What am I gonna do?" you asked,
& the only thing you could think to do was run away fast...

What? How could you leave me? You knew I couldn't handle this on my own
I wanted this baby to grow up within a family & a happy home
Though it wasn't in the plans, I felt a love for you that made it hard for me to even stand
I thought this would bring us closer together, I thought you would be a bigger man...

But now you want to run away, as if you didn't have anything to do with this?
Who is going tell this baby that her father doesn't believe it exists?
Thinking you couldn't hack it, my mother told me I shouldn't have it,
so I had the operation this morning & our baby vanished like some kind of evil magic
I feel guilty as hell, I don't even sleep anymore
I walked into a night of unprotected passion, right into a world of lonely & closed doors
My father's still looking for you, so don't think you're getting off free
I hope he kills you for breaking my heart, tearing us apart, & destroying our family...

Wait....you robbed me of the chance to enjoy life
Because you couldn't control yourself for 1 night
You robbed me of the chance to love, to be loved & to make love
God chooses when it's time to go, who gave you the power to judge?
You also robbed me of the chance to breathe
It seemed as soon as I walked through the door of life, it was my turn to leave
Why didn't I have any say in this?
Who made you the writer of my life's script?
You never considered the fact I had feelings too
I couldn't wait for you to hold me in your arms, just to be 1 with you
I just find it hard to believe you couldn't find a way to make things work
How long did it take for you to make the final decision, how bad did it hurt?
I know you feel like my spirit is haunting you constantly,
but I just want to know why my life had to end because you didn't act responsibly.

SEPTEMBER LOVE

As I woke up that morning, all I could do was think about my baby coming home
She had been out of town all week on business & I was home all alone
You see, we'd been together for over 2 years & I had without question knew what it meant to be in love
Since she's come into my life, I've learned to listen, be patient & found out what being a better man was
I spent most of the morning preparing for her arrival, it was difficult for my nerves to settle
I wanted to set up the perfect proposal, to show her I was ready to take it to the next level
I had hidden the ring in the back corner of the dresser, I knew she would never find it there
I couldn't wait to see her face once she saw what I had prepared
I had arranged for a limo to pick her up from the airport in about an hour
so I knew I had to take care of some last minute details & quickly hop in the shower
From there, all I could do was nervously wait
I noticed I missed a call when I was in the shower, I forgot I had my phone on vibrate
I checked my voicemail & soon realized I had missed a call from my baby
I figured her flight was delayed or her bags were missing, it was always something crazy
She greeted me as usual saying, "Hey babe," her voice sounding sweet as ever
"I can't wait to get home to you, so that we can be together
Being with you is everything I've imagined a perfect life would be
but right now, my love, I'm afraid to say, the unthinkable is happening to me
I feel as if I'm in a horrible dream. This will be kind of difficult to explain,
but I was just awakened by several men trying to hijack my plane...

I don't know what's going on, I just want you to know that I'm not afraid
I am counting on faith to help me through this, just know that I have already prayed
Hold on a second....
1 of the hijackers just walked passed my seat
I don't want him to know I'm on the phone, so I'll have to whisper when I speak
I want you to know that I knew about your proposal, you never could keep a secret
I found the ring in the back of the dresser, that was a terrible place to keep it
I know how hard you have been working on your surprise, I could tell you were stressed
I am so anxious to hear your proposal, but right now love, I am under duress
And if it is God's will that I make it through this mess
I want you to know that my answer is yes
If I don't make it, just know that you are the man of my dreams
You have been....
I know it's difficult to hear me over all of the screams
I wish I could hear your voice.
I know I'd feel much more at ease
I need to hear 1 of your jokes, you were always such a tease
I'm okay though, I'll just imagine walking down the aisle with you
with all of our family & friends witnessing our union, can't you picture it too?
Wait a minute baby....
it feels like the plane is starting to go down
Please tell my parents goodbye & remember I lov........."
I never heard another sound

04
Love Infinite

True love is eternal, infinite, and always like itself. It is equal and pure, without violent demonstrations

- Honore de Belzac

SINGLE FATHER

You have all heard of deadbeat dads, no good n--- & baby daddies

But what about me?

Every morning I fix breakfast, braid hair & get my baby girl ready for the day
I make sure she washes her face & brushes her teeth. I kiss her cheeks & when she leaves me
I pray
I pray that when she's at school
she gains the knowledge she needs
I pray when she's at church
she finds the faith to know she will succeed

Yes, we do go to church.
I want her to know that in all things, put God 1st
I also tell her that no man can determine her worth
I help her with her homework & teach her right from wrong
When she has nightmares, I sing her to sleep with her favorite song

So what about me?

No, all men are not the same
& though society may have you believe I don't exist, forever devoted & dedicated to her, I will remain
I stepped up when her mother decided she wouldn't bother
I am a man of God, a man who loves his daughter....

 I am a single father

DEAR MYRLIE

Dear Myrlie,

I see you're still standing strong, looking beautiful as ever
I wish I were there with you, so we could enjoy life together
I guess in our minds, we knew the day would come, but neither of us could foresee
that the Lord would call me up on high that summer in '63
I always think about our times in Mississippi & all the struggles we went through
It feels good to know that even while I'm gone, through you the fight continues
I talk to Martin all of the time. We still believe that one day, we SHALL overcome
A lot has changed since the past, but there's still a lot of work to be done
Thank DeLaughter for sacrificing his life & for helping to let justice reign
If it weren't for him, the thought of a retrial would never have been entertained
& please, say hello to Darrell, Reena, & James
Tell them I love them & that I'm proud they are there to live out my name
Forgive Beckwith, but don't forget the dreams that I left with
Think about the love we were blessed with & use that to carry out our message
Finally, when times get rough, remember it will never be too hard to find me
I will always be with you, so just seek God, & he will help you set your mind free

With love,
Medgar

1600

When I decided to take on this position
I needed encouragement from you & you listened
When the opposition was trying to tear me down,
your strength kept my feet on solid ground
I am often times forced to make tough decisions,
from abortion, to terrorism, to racial division
Though the country may be at war
it is only for you my heart truly fights for
When I come home to you & the kids, I never feel more secure
More security than any secret serviceman could ever ensure
Your love brings diplomacy to my soul
Just when I feel like throwing in the towel, you push me to stick to my goals
You have stayed by my side through it all
through my mistakes & through my fears, you are the rock that won't allow me to fall
Some would consider me the leader of the free world, but nothing brings me more joy than my 3 girls
As president, I solemnly swear, that I will faithfully execute the duties of being your man
If anyone is to ever question whether our love will stand,
I would simply respond by saying…"Yes, we can."

GOD FATHER

You are more than just my best friend's child
There is a whole lot more to the innocence in your smile
Last night it hit me, if tomorrow my best friend should leave,
you would become my responsibility
God forbid, but if that day should ever occur
I would be that shoulder you could lean on that could never be deterred
I would welcome you like an angel with open arms
Like a knight in shining armor, I would give my life, to shield you from harm
I will answer any of life's questions you want to ask
If it is God's will, I would pray for strength to complete this task
There is no boundary to the things I would do
No matter what wrong you may have done, should you ever need someone, remember I will always be here for you

GRANDMAMMA

You gave birth to a generation & many more to come
You embody wisdom & strength to all of your daughters & sons
You are the ambassador of love & the centerpiece of this family
You symbolize hope & the promise of everything we plan to be
You have earned the title of queen & your crown will reign eternally
You have shown me anything is possible & have lit a fire that constantly burns in me
You have experienced things in life that we could never imagine or dream to see
We can only pray that you are proud of all that we've done & hope to be
We can't express through words all that you are & all you have been in just 1 statement
This is just a simple dedication to a beautiful angel; there will never be a replacement

9 MONTHS

To the lady who would give her last dime
The lady who would give her life at anytime
With every sacrifice, you inspire me
You gave me the choice to be whoever I wanted to be
You lifted me when I felt I had no reason to stand
You showed me how a woman expects to be treated by her man
You introduced me to God & shared your spirit with me
Your faith has defined love eternally
All I can say is thank you, knowing I could never repay you for all you have done
Hopefully these words will express how much I love & appreciate you....

    Love,

     Your son

LITTLE ANGEL

You were truly an angel, even before your time
& the Lord called you to heaven so the whole world could see you shine
Right now, this is something that no one can even begin to understand
we just have to find peace in knowing that you are no longer in pain in God's hands
So many sweet memories you have left behind
I will never be able to get your beautiful smile out of my mind
I would do anything in this world to see you walk through the door again
There are so many things that I want to say, I wouldn't even know where to begin
I know you are in heaven, riding your brand new bike, living life without a care in the world
How could we have known that God would bring so many blessings through such a beautiful little girl?
You are my little angel & I need you to keep watching over me
When I'm down, I will feel better knowing that you are standing close to me
We will miss you so much, even though we know your soul is at peace
Just promise you will keep smiling down on me until the day our souls once again meet

OUR FATHER

I pray these words meet you with sincerity
I am at a point in my life where I need clarity
Long days & short nights, the stress at times does not seem fair
Trying to hold on to the fact that you will not give me more than I can bear
Without a restful moment to spare, I offer up to you this prayer
When I find myself in the midst of despair, I know hope is out there somewhere
It's probably out there with my faith, which I often lose during the storm
Or maybe it is with my spirit, which is constantly broken & torn
I feel ashamed when I complain, because I know so many going through much worse
I put the job, the relationship, & the family on the frontline, instead of putting you 1st
However, whatever the situation, you continue to bless me still
I had to understand, my loved ones going to heaven was all part of your will
You are the counselor, the lawyer & the lover, wearing the shoes no other can wear
No matter what corner I turn or road I choose, you are always there
You always shine down on me & forgive me, even when I don't necessarily do as you please
You always bestow your blessings upon me, even on those nights I forget to get down on my knees
You continue to support me, even when I put you to the side
You spared my life, that night I should've died
You dried my eyes when she made me cry
You were the money when I ran low on my supply
I don't deserve anything you give
How dare I not praise you every day I live?
Yet, I ask you for strength & mercy as I try to go about living life through you
Continue to watch over me & keep me, & let your blessings fall through

                                        Amen

THE END

An Abstrakk creation

J. Gralyn Stokes
@jgralyn_official

Writer, poet, and educator was born in Greensboro, North Carolina but reared in Richmond, Virginia. He is a former elementary school teacher for the City of Richmond Public Schools and an Old Dominion University alum. He developed a passion for writing in middle school, and learned to appreciate the power of language being inspired by the works of Langston Hughes, Nikki Giavanni, and music from musician/songwriters Stevie Wonder, Kirk Franklin and Jay-Z.

Gralyn also developed a passion for web design and graphic arts. He launched Abstrakk Ink, a graphic design and creative arts company in 2019. He plans to pursue his passion for the arts through a series of children's books, short stories, novels and also developing short films.

Vol 1 is a collection of poems written between 1996 and 2010. I always had dreams of being a published author and one day having my words available to the world. Saying; "I'll get to it tomorrow" or waiting for the perfect time wasn't going to help me get to where I wanted to be. I had seen too many examples of how tomorrow wasn't guaranteed. One day I woke up and put away the excuses, dedicated the summer to getting my book published.

Life happens. Allowing fear to alter your focus and desire for something greater is a tragedy in itself. May this book inspire you to take the first step. Put away the excuses and stop procrastinating toward your destiny.

www.ingramcontent.com/pod-product-compliance
Lightning Source LLC
LaVergne TN
LVHW041543060526
838200LV00037B/1114